Visible Ink

Poems by
George Starbuck

Edited by
Kathryn Starbuck and Elizabeth Meese

THE UNIVERSITY OF ALABAMA PRESS
TUSCALOOSA & LONDON

Visible Ink

poems • George Starbuck

9 8 7 6 5 4 3 2 1
10 09 08 07 06 05 04 03 02

Designer: Michele Myatt Quinn
Typeface: Courier and Syntax

∞

The paper on which this book is printed meets the minimum requirements of
American National Standard for Information Science–Permanence of Paper for
Printed Library Materials, ANSI Z39.48-1984.

Library of Congress Cataloging-in-Publication Data

Starbuck, George, 1931–1996
    Visible Ink / George Starbuck; edited by Kathryn Starbuck and Elizabeth Meese.
        p.   cm.
    ISBN 0-8173-1154-8 (cloth: alk. paper) — ISBN 0-8173-1155-6 (pbk: alk. paper)
    I. Starbuck, Kathryn, 1939– II. Meese, Elizabeth A., 1943– III. Title.
    PS3569.T3356 V57 2002 811'.54—dc21

                                                            2001005917

British Library Cataloguing-in-Publication Data available

Grateful acknowledgment is made to the following publications in which these
poems appeared:
    *The American Poetry Review, The Atlantic Monthly, Bedford Introduction to
Literature, The Breadloaf Anthology of Contemporary Poetry, Grand Street, Harper s,
The Iowa Review, Kenyon Review, Key West Review, The Laurel Review, New Let-
ters, The New Yorker, The Ohio Review, Partisan Review, Ploughshares, POETRY,
Southwest Review, Tri-Quarterly.*
    We are grateful to the many people who generously assisted us with this
book. We wish especially to thank Nicole Mitchell and the entire staff of The Uni-
versity of Alabama Press for their precision and initiative. We are grateful as well
for the assistance of Amanda Page.
                                                        K. S. and E. M.

for George Starbuck's children—
Meg, Steve, John, Tony, and Josh

Contents

Introduction

These George Starbuck poems were written, widely published, and anthologized from the early 1980s to the early 1990s. George had often spoken of his *Visible Ink* manuscript and given public readings from it. In fact, when he died, he left three manila folders, all versions of *Visible Ink*.

In each folder, he included many examples of his favorite and final formal invention—a form he took particular delight in employing and varying—something he called Standard Length and Breadth Sonnets, or SLABS for short. They are fourteen-line poems, with fourteen unspaced characters per line, which form a dense slab on the page. The SLABS and all the poems in this volume reflect George's unique lifelong habits of pursuing his obsessions with war, beebop, vout, crazy word endings (in many languages), American demotic, quarks, whimsy, mathematical games, and what he saw as the eternal beauties of physics.

As is perhaps inevitable with posthumous works, standard questions have arisen. I have been asked to make plain what parts of this book are as George left them and what parts, if any, we altered in preparing the manuscript. George died in August of 1996 before he decided which poems to include in his final book and what their order should be. He called himself fortunate to have completed what mattered most to him: the individual poems. The summer he died, he told me if I ever felt inclined to form the poems into a collection, simply to try to see that the manuscript was suitably pruned and shaped. (There he was, talking once again like the tireless vegetable gardener and tree-grower he had been during our two decades in New Hampshire.)

For several years, I let the folders of poems marked "Visible

Ink" sit safe in our home while waiting for the courage to enter them. In the middle distance, I could see George in his final years toying with various ways of presenting the manuscript. (When he could not focus on this, he would turn to work on a large box of never finished palindrome poems.) It got to the point where only the forces of grief and inertia held me back. Last summer, when The University of Alabama Press expressed a desire to publish George's work, the time at last felt exactly right to prepare a collection. I invited his friend, the critic Elizabeth Meese, to work with me in editing this book. Her dedication has helped turn this into an altogether rewarding and vibrant task.

One day, as I anticipated Elizabeth's arrival at my home for a work session, I found myself in a dusty hallway closet dragging out all the heavy leaves of the sturdy oak harvest table that George and I had bought at an Amish farm auction outside Iowa City in the first year of our marriage. I thought I had put away those old leaves for good when he died. I assembled the table to its room-filling eleven-foot length. I placed the poems upon it. I wondered which would be chosen for the indelible arrangement, which would be returned to rest invisible in the manila folders at The University of Alabama's W. S. Hoole Special Collections Library. I began playing with choosing, then ordering the poems. I had fun.

For the next several months, Elizabeth and I walked round and round that enormous table as we made the selections and shaped *Visible Ink* into the book it has become. George and I had played this game of musical poems many times in the 1970s and 1980s as he gathered the poems for *Desperate Measures,* for *The Argot Merchant Disaster,* and for other books; we often had a big tableful of poems to contemplate and discuss over supper as he selected works for public readings. Again and again, in working on this book, I found myself shocked and guided by implanted as well as dug up memories.

In addition, Elizabeth drew upon notes from several meetings she had with George in the winter of 1994 when they discussed the full body of his work. Thus we combined what we knew—or what we thought we knew—and simply made the choices. We were strengthened and often amazed by the fact that we both independently, almost invariably—almost eerily—came to the same conclusion about poems and placement.

Of course we did not make any changes or impose revisions on the poems themselves. None. When we found more than one version of the same poem, we chose what we knew to be the final version when we knew it, with a weighted preference for the published version when applicable. We corrected typographical errors. We checked a number of spellings, some of which are decidedly idiosyncratic, then left them as George had made them.

I had the joy and good fortune of living for three decades amidst the love and bountiful harvest of George Starbuck's mind and art. It now pleases me that his unique voice is again made public and visible as we present *Visible Ink*.

A year from now, we plan to offer a large collection containing exemplary poems from all of his books showing a lifetime's work from the 1950s to the 1990s. It is titled *The Works*.

Kathryn Starbuck, Tuscaloosa, Summer 2001

Visible Ink

ON AN URBAN BATTLEFIELD

Shopper and shopper, grocer and grocer.
Sidewalk delicatessen. Crouch and eat.

Party-of-God? So be it. Posher-but-kosher-
but-consecrated? You got it. In pieces? Neat.

There is no death but death. Hear, worshipers.
Same lockstep with a hesitation wrinkle to the beat.

I take the pollster's tack and the upholsterer's.
You need a pricetag and a tally sheet?

When I said battlefield when I said shoppers,
what did your fury seize upon as meat?

Which snapshot leapt up first? Which flitch which swatch?
Did you envision Kitcheners complete

with self-inflicted quirt-strokes to their jodhpurs?
I am your troubadour. I am discreet.

A jolly Russky ribboned up for openers?
Hush; you shall have him. Harvested like wheat.

S.D.I.

It's nice up here in Air
Force One. I get to wear
my gold-braid baseball cap
and stand before the map
of New El Salvador
and point out which came first
our game of chicken or
the other guy's and burst
into a sob because
I have this reverence
about the selfless dead
and when the audience
gets rolling something does
this curtsy with my head.

TO A REAL STANDUP PIECE
OF PAINTED CROCKERY

I wonder what the Greeks kept in these comicstrip canisters.
Plums, milletseed, incense, henna, oregano.
Speak to me, trove. Tell me you contained dried smoked tongue
    once.
Or a sorcerer or a cosmetologist's powders and unguents.
And when John Keats looked at you in a collection of pots
it was poetry at first sight: quotable beautiful
teleological concatenations of thoughts.

It's the proverbial dog of a poem, though:
slobbering panting and bright-eyed like a loquacious thug
or a spokesperson embattled on behalf of a sociopolitical thesis*
to which he has not had access owing to the need-to-know basis.

And he never says which pot. Just an oasis
of tease in a sea of tilth, kind of a concrete catachresis
bopping along with timbrels, irrepressible as Count Basie,
fabulous I mean classic I mean vout,
keeping the buckwheat in and the weevils out
while the rest of us get and spend and ache and earn
and go to the Bruce Springsteen concert and take our turn
lining up at the Metropolitan to look at the Macedonian gold
    krater
and promising ourselves to read up seriously.

*(Beauty : Truth = Ignorance : Bliss). Consult Précis.

3

SLABS FOR GEORGE HERBERT

```
AtLeastItsNotA
Synchrostrobic
GizmoWithDials
OnItIKnowIKnow
IvePutYouInIt&
SomeFolksFindA
StandardLength
&BreadthSonnet
Claustrophobic

SoTryAnAerobic
ExerciseOrTwoI
MeanBreatheAah
BreatheSeeIsnt
ThatSomeRelief
```

RUDE COT

AllSoulsGhosts
InfestGilsonSt

GoblinsDoTheir
AntiOgnissanti

LetsTurnOutThe
LightOohQuaint

RudeItMayBeBut
AntiromanticIt
AintWeGotLoaf&
Poem&CaseOfNew
AntichiChianti

SureAmGladImAn
Antitransubst-
antiationalist

STREET CRIES

New lamps. New imports in the wineshop windows.
Three Tommies halfway window-shopping ("Whores.")
Pitiful damnedest bunch of merchandisers
Trying to do some business in the stores.

Two sizes of inflated Santa Clauses.
Poor Ireland, with these cheeky ruddy blimps
Elbowing for your five-year-olds' attention.
The five-year-olds hang back. They ape their elders.
The seven-year-olds stand around in clumps.

The cuddly cult of darling Baby Jesus
Seeps wordlessly around them and replaces
The Saints, the Mariolatry, the gore.
The priests are gentler than they were before.
I'm not against American improvements.

In daylight, down a side street, not an alley,
A bunch of little men is making cocktails.
Huddled around like nine-year-olds at marbles.
High holiday. Old bottles for old scores.
One holds a rag in readiness. One pours.

The eldest could be going on eleven.
He lines the bottles up to get them even.
Only a stranger to this Bible scene
Would think to look for children of thirteen.

OYSTER BAR ON THE ROAD TO MURURUA

It's Bruce Lee, last of the Chieu Hois.
Taro reading: the Haoles are losing their pois.
The barfed-on offer their excusez-mois
Hey hey. Thanks for the memo. Un; deux; trois;

Banjoist kotoist jingoist Maoist Hoist,
the one-man all-girl hula group gets bois-
trouser and boistrouser half Piaf half ois-
eau-lyre half Rose La Rose half Blanche Dubois.

Not half bad for a honky-junkie-bourgeois
novelty act from Winnetka, Illinois.
Fabulous quick split. Great pair of borzois.
Woh woh the way she wears that car-wash chamois.

But clue me in. Envoi to end envois.

Is that you under the grass skirt, François?
I know it's one big commie-racist-judeois-
lamic plot out there but make me its connois-
seur. Is it Christo back from dying the Simois

red? Does he giftwrap Diamond Head? Is it Lois
Lane to the rescue? Are these cold-stoned Iroquois
part of the schmeer? Am I getting the patois?
After we ticket Greenpeace do we hoist

anchor again for the dreaded Marco Is.?
Are we the head-on of the hoi polloi
while the great brains in basements hunch like Korchnois
or just a late-night case of the 2001s?

DYLAN: THE LIMERICK

There was an old man from Duluth.
He used to be took for some youth,
        So he wheezed and he hacked
        And he hyped up his act
To be twenty times truer than truth.

He did his Old-Man-Memphis
Empathy-with-emphys-
        Ema schmooze.
Did his minstrel Ham-And-Shem fuss.
Did THE OLD MAN'S ABM FAC-
ILITY DEEMPHAS-
        IS BY DEMOLITION BLUES.
        He brung the teenyboppers their bad news

A la Kali. A la Baal.
A la shoot-out at the A-OK Corral.
        Bimbobamboozeler
        Pseudomethuselah
Groupiegropin' Grampap in a Mafia LaSalle

He was sharper than a serpent's tooth
An apotheosis of uncouth
        So redolently schlocky
        Insatiable Bacchae
Demolished the Apollo ticket booth.

ANOTHER PHOTO-OP IN THE SUDAN

You want dead? You want a bandana'd Danaid
spooning out soup to skulls? You want Bob (Live Aid)
Geldof detonating? Come to Abu Daid.

Please. We are the stinking rich. Ultraid-
ealism makes us contraid-
eological. Please. We have come to Abu Daid.

Bully for you old dear like the mermaid said.
You and the Church and the Dergue and the A.I.D.
taking the rag and the talcum to Abu Daid.

We can be God, we can be last man assegai'd.
We can deliver New Hampshire and have it bonsai'd.
We can be hopeless and loaded and get waylaid.
We can be wealth to, be welcome to, Abu Daid.

You can be in the Uffizi. The Thebaid.
Back and forth over the panel the adventures braid.
Pink face, brown cowl, gray mule, in a green green plaid.
Chromosome. Vade-mecum. To Abu Daid.

But Geldof. Mad mahout to this Aida.
Tries anything. A taste of his Adida.
A grandstand tantrum a la Idi Dada.
He has kedged clawed backpacked Dakota'd Hyundai'd
mountains. And they have come to Abu Daid.

SONGS FOR THE OLD NEW JERSEY
SHELLING THE SHOUF

Spads Krags battleships howitzers those were the good old days.
    Bangeloring the barbed wire. Setting ablaze
Armored patrols of jack-in-the-boxes, watching the contents pop
    Up and go galloping, writhe, crackle and stop.
And then the good old sing-along at the Malmedy canteen,
Oasis in a no-man's-land of corpses turning green,
Where the booze was booze, and the basketcases gathered in a
        ring
To join the whores and orderlies and corporals and sing:

"Pikes dirks falchionets scatterguns those were the good old days.
To see the man that strangles you. To see the bastard's gaze
    Intensify, go desperate, and glaze.
And the grapeshot and the cavalry exploding through the haze.
Damn, Sacrebleu, Zounds, Teufel but wasn't that the nuts:
Sticking a pig of a Gascon in his piggery of guts
And trooping all off later to be brave inebriates
And sing the soldier ballad while you drain the Malmsey butts:

"Brands rams javelins catapults cauldrons of boiling oil.
Crosses against the infidel. Alhambras to despoil.
Whole citadels escorted to a torchlight Exodus.
      Whole tribes, Hey Nonny Nonny with a heinousness
      Unparalleled since Darius's days
Those were the winds of widowmaking *those* were the fields of
    praise
When war was fucking war by fucking Christ and men were men
And dawn still found us caroling and singing once again:

"Rocks prods mastadon-mandibles those were the good old days.
    Heads to be bashed, liver-and-lights to braise
And pass among the warriors in order of blood rank
Before the commonality of merrymakers drank
The bloodred blood of victory and chug-a-lugged along
    Beside the ancient chieftain's dance and song:
"Kicks to the jaw! Knees to the testicles! Teeth to the jugular!"
The song of how it used to be before the forests were
    Brought down and the great god took up the club
    And rucksack of the churl Beelzebub.

ELIOT RUNS ON

DiscoingLately
Disconsolately
InAnAbandonedA
FrameByTheSeaI
DidNotThinkThe
GoGosSpokeToMe

Discouragingly
CrassAndJingly
&TheHyannisMTV
Inconstant&The
WindsPhilately

Discomfitingly
TinglyLikeAWan
Discountoutlet
Counterpersons
DiscontinuousT
GroupTalkathon

UP TO HERE
WITH THE PIED
PIPERS OF GOTHAM

```
IDontLikeMimeI
DontLikeSleaze
IDontLikeSteel
BandSymphonies
Psalterypawing
SlobsLikeThese
Discountenance
Philanthropies

NorAmIAvidToBe
EyeballedOddly
ByAnIdleRibald
OboistWhoFlaps
APiebaldMotley
WhilstHeTweets
```

THE ENCHANTED GLADE

The old days. What a life.
Bards barded. Rhyme was rife.
A farthing for a vocal,
And each and every yokel
Became a singing bird.

The yeoman plied his yerd.
The rhymster chimed concordance.
The druid at his war dance,
The monk at his devotions,
The suitor, his emotions
Deliciously deranged,
Got with it and exchanged
The contents of their purses
For made-to-measure verses
To terrify the Huns with,
Debauch a bunch of nuns with,
Or both at one fell swoop.
It was a jolly troupe,
The customers of rhyme.
Love-sonnets were a dime
A dozen. So were steaks.
The dead get all the breaks.
The big consumer craze
Was ribald roundelays
In Hudibrastic couplets.
It sure beats printing up LET'S
BOOGIE bumper stickers.
The hangdog banjo-pickers
Of Albion could choose
From half a hundred hues

And ten degrees of luster
From out-and-out gut-buster
To whispered spectral wail.
But thereby hangs a cautionary tale.

It fell upon a day
In Lammastide, the way
So many episodes
Keep falling in the odes
Surviving from the period.
A maker of a myriad
Of madrigals, the Barry
Manilow and Gary
Snyder of his age
(Preceded by a page
And jugglers in procession)
Was plying his profession
The best way he knew how.
Some think he had been hexed because a cow
Had bleated in his path.
At any rate the wrath
Of something must have struck,
Or he just had phenomenal bad luck.

He was, as was his wont,
Extemporizing. Don't
Imagine something scuzzy
Or slapdash just because he
Didn't have a script.
The couplets fairly dripped
With lyric ornament.
Whole bestiaries went
Bananas to provide
A moment's versified

Illustrative material.
Whole glittering aethereal
Kathismata, replete
With deities in sweet
Olympian repose,
Came tumbling when he chose
To hustle things along
By calling down the gods to do the song.

The faster he proceeded,
The featlier he speeded.
This cat was in the pink.
Unstoppable. You'd think
With all the thee-and-thouing,
Ywissing and I-trowing,
Thou-dosting and he-dothing,
A poet would get nothing
But megrims for his pains.
You'd think an olden English minstrel's brains
With all that extra grammar
Would have took up the hammer
And chisel and cried "Out!"
You'd think he would have turned into a lout
With porridge in his beard.

Yet here he was, a weird
Coherence to his ravings.
And here they came, their savings
Ajingle in their fists,
His abject gang of groupie-lutanists.
He reveled in his prowess.
To show the yokels how es-
Pecially delicious
A flat and inauspicious

Subject could become,
He launched, ad libitum,
One last improvisation:
A rhyme in celebration
Of Rhyme. It went like this:

"Good countrymen, ywis
We take great things for granted.
We know God never scanted
Us wind and wold and wave.
We thank Him, that He gave
The bog, the holt, the heather,
To heap, against the weather,
A crofter's good hearth fire.
All vitals we require—
Space, Power, Substance, Time—
He lavishes. But best of all is Rhyme.

"For what if rhyme got scant?
Would gallants gallivant
Through battlefield and boudoir?
A vexed hex would hoodoo our
Impassionedest pursuits
And leave us lallygagging like galoots.

"And if rhyme got still scanter?
The palliative banter
Young duchesses require
Might stumble, flutter, crepitate, expire.

"If rhyme got really scarce,

"If rhyme got really scarce,"

(A whole-line repetition
Is right in the tradition
Of mainstream Dirty Blues
And proper for a troubadour to use.

But this long breath he draws?
This *second* Pregnant Pause?
A horrid thought was dawning.)
His retinue, nine fawning
Bards' Guild apprentices,
Were suddenly abuzz.
Their master, posed as though
To mouth one mighty mot,
Whirled, with a Hellish look,
And in the nonce it took
To send a laser burn
Through each of them in turn,
Hissed out, "Okay, you guys,
I don't want alibis,
I want a rhyme for scarce."

Somebody thought up vers
Libre and on they went,
But it had been a sobering event.

FILMS TRIP
COMICSTRIP
COLUMN VS.
KRAZY KAEL

1

SheTellsMeCome-
dyHasMadeACome-
backSheSezCome
Look
    ImASitcomE-
clecticSoICome
LopingLikeSome
Shnook&Yup

        Come-
dianPlanksCome-
dienneBopsCome-
diansGetsACome-
uppanceAndCome-
downOh
    OW
      ZOK
        MMM
ItsaRockmSockm
ItsTitCity
      Come-
dyByScriptComm-
itteeWhereCome
sTheMotto&Come
TheOutcomeCome
RainOrComeCome-
ts&Bombs

2

        Come,
Powell&Loy
        Come-
dyGotBroke
        Come
DoItAgain

        OCome-
hitheriestComes-
tible&SlyCome-
dienne

        ONarcome-
thodicalIncomp-
oopHerSot

        ACome-
onToGetWelcome
In&Not
        ANewcome-
nEngineOrEcome-
chanicalVacuum
PistonPump

        Come
Gleam

3

        &LocoMe
NoLocosIfISeem

```
Aleak&Overcome
Yes
      Comma
             Cccome
SdHeIsAnEECumm-
ingsClassicOMe
OMyEvenTheComm-
édiaAndTheComé-
dieHumaineCome
OnAllRosy&Come-
ly&Sexmad&Come-
dicLikeTheCome-
dalistsInACome-
fest&Maybe


            Come-
dyKnowsHowCome
GismIsOakum


             Cum
Ça


   ItsAComicOme-
let


   VivaQueCome
```

Note: Rhyme is, of course, an impurity—one of the grossest. Hell, all "prosodic form" is an impurity. We're lucky to have the whole history of Western literatures to remind us of that, while reveling in our fringe lit and fringe lingo and taking our guilty incurable delight in rap, sonnet, Clerihew, all that impedimenta.

So, what I've tossed in your hopper is the most egregiously overrhymed (and over*non*rhymed) thing I had. It's bedizened toad. But heartfelt.

PRACTICAL SHOOTER COMES
TO DOWNERS GROVE

They've took my Mach-10 Special.
       They've took Dad's Remingtons.
When they get Bubba's, only
       The in-laws will have guns.

Saturday night's a longshot
       Contraption as it is.
A man without a Magnum's
       A piece of agribiz.

He might as well push daisies
       And model for a wreath
And pick a granite afghan
       To cuddle up beneath.

You've seen the streets of Berwyn
       In the county name of Cook.
We're talkin' cold survival.
       We're talkin' donnybrook.

What if a drunk accosts you
       And mouths an ethnic slur?
What if your wife takes refuge
       And you catch up with her?

It's people that kill people,
       An people's bustin' west
Out of the inner suburbs
       Like they was air-expressed.

It isn't just lost hardware
            And that they got no right.
It's the humiliation.
            You take last Tuesday night:

There in my bed defenseless,
            Woke up at three a.m.
And up the stair come footsteps.
            It had to have been them.

I was a sitting target
            Disarmed by liberals.
Ransacked my bedside table
            And all I found was pills.

You see the situation?
            You see the price of it?
A thousand drowsing suburbs
            Just waitin' to be hit.

What if it had been baddies
            And not Great Aunt Irene?
What if the one split-second
            When they're behind the screen

And I'm where I can zero
            Their shadow-image in
And they can't see who's pumpin'
            Their bellies full of tin

Goes by, in dumb frustration,
            While I'm still gropin' for
The family peacekeeper
            That I ain't got no more?

I tell you there'd be henchmen
        Emboldened by my death
Rampagin' into Downers
        Before you get your breath.

(It takes a heap o' henchmen
        To give them hophead hoods
The yellowdog bravado
        To raid the neighborhoods.

It takes a heap o' henchmen
        In winrows up the stairs
Now-and-then, to remind 'em
        The country just ain't theirs.)

You think about your houses.
        You think about your wives.
You think about the access
        To ten-inch carving knives

And Lizzie Borden hat pins
        And side arms of their own
Among the rougher classes.
        Next time you hear the phone

Click off, because you answered
        In your best Eastwood voice,
You think about it, Mister.
        You only got one choice.

Stonewall 'em, like the heroes
        And braves of long ago.
A man don't need a castle
        To have an Alamo.

DURNDEST THING

WellShredMySox
AnCallMeShorty
ItWasOllieBaba
TheOnemanForty
WinksCommittee
DidThemDeeds&I
NivverHadAClue

HereIBeenTryin
EverDodgeIKnew
FromDontCallMe
IshmaelIllCall
UtoYabaDabaEli
EliAliasCallMe
Irresponsible2

AMAZING GRACIOUS LIVING ON I-93

I've read the propaganda,
and I believe it now.
I shoulda bought a van de-
signed to squush a cow.
Small cars are "unforgiving."
They crumple up like foam.
It takes a heap o' mortgage
to have a heap o' home,
and if a heap o' heap'll
satisfy some people,
then who am I to holler?

They musta paid top dollar
to furnish a machine
for live-in demolition
derby competition
with stained-glass picture windshield
and *Playboy* Magazine
entablature. I mean
my little thirteen-inch-wheeled
Rabbit must feel queer
to find me stopping here
to contemplate the roadside
without a HoJo's near.

I mean I've got some odes I'd
like to finish yet
before I make another
bunny silhouette
along the fuselage
of someone's ten-ton Taj

Mahalmobile. Good brother,
that comes a little steep.
I like this highway shoulder.
Just sittin'. Gittin' older.
I like it a whole heap.

ERRAND AT THE LONE TREE MALL

This gizmo to spin spin-
aches aches to be mine.

It's a high-speed disco-disco-
very, very expensive, very fine.

I want it, and I want a set of ten-pound cast-iron bundts.
I want to have a kitchen with some *stuff* in it for once.

Great rough-hewn rivetty skillets.
Badge Oak cheeseboard and steak-knife sets.

Blowing a wad but who cares, cares-
sing (sing
twiddle kadiddle kachoong)

its digital widgets its rotary gadgets

for slivering almonds and slurrying celery
Diggety dog I got doodads here. Make room.

Miss Checkout, with her loom
gone suddenly berserk
as if it were Penelope's
and data tapes were tapes-

tries tries
bonking it but bonking it won't work.

Smiles. Shrugs. Geez.
à la lavender-vendor only wants to tease

out and then bestow
a beautiful
empurpled pale memento.

Poor damsel of romance.

She needs a champion and here's my chance
to be her pal her paladin her hero O

make it a cash transaction what's the dif.

She can't believe I said that. What a dimwit. What a stiff.

She shrugs, looks heavenward for her directions,

a Tex-Mex Joan-of-Arc in milkwhite buckskins,
alamode Alamodelivery livery
chased and ornate beyond posses' possessing,
sing jingle sing jangle a she-sheriff riff.
Bonks it again. *Mirabile.* Good news.
My charge slip: eggplant purple on pale blues.
My loading platform call slips in coördinated hues.
Whole psychedelic
spectrum of delic-
ious IOUS.

I scoop up and skedaddle. No I don't.
Now I got to pass the x-and-o hunt.
Worse than assessment days at nursery school.

The competition, paragons of cool,
stopped and slapped with a Star Wars scorecard
only a droid could read read-
just just marvelously. No sweat.

Scan for the squiggle. Set
Bic to ballot and trust in MCI.

A dollyful of mannequins whips by.
Watch it, if they make contact with an eye.

The new Club-Med Medusa USA.

The smoldering, deep-shadowed, cloisonné
look of a lady-of-Endor endorsing
(sing poke it and pack it, punk)

the autosuggestive the autopsy-
chic the seamy the dreamy the demise-
dated the drunk.

Askance and askancer
(don't ask and don't answer)
teleportated, they teeter through,
bound for another department. And vanished. Phew.

No mayhem in the Mall.
Just quick, subliminal
riffles and feeding-frenzies everywhere.

One smurf one Junior Miss one striding rare
Saturday doll with an odalisque air
and the lacquerwork of an Ingres ingressing
(sing singlefile Injunstyle whisperless quick)
straight for the tables where superfantastic

hawser-humongous cableknit cardigans,
Labradorean lobstermen's pullovers,
ultradimensional Gordian oodles

of made-in-Jamaica macramé-mimicry
cry to be hefted and sported and bunched and hugged.

Amazons half-diaphanous, half-shagrugged.

I look up and I'm there. I'm at my errand.

Blackness where a Krugerrand
snuggles on its little mouselike pouch.
And in the place of honor?
Gone. Spent.

Token of Incan incan-
descent descent.

Not Atahualpa's. Not Pizarro's either.
Some bad hidalgo gives the guards a breather
and swirls his cape, and takes a token fix,
and owns a demon rescued from the mix
of demons in King Carlos' melting pot.

I'd like to have been there. The fiendish glee.

I think the look of him looks back at me,
complicit. Every crammed-in ingot got
cartage to Cartagena, naval escort to Cadiz.
And God is mighty, and the worm got his.
And if the sea rose up, miraculous . . .

Primitive Prospero. Prosperous us.

Whose voice this is that hustles me from twenty
videoscreens at once, I think I know.
He comes into my home when I get lonely

and I don't mind the line of bull. It's only
natural natural gas gassing
Sing hey for the loyal few
drilling out here in the channel bringing you

beautiful oceans of bloo-bloobloobloob-loobloob,
beautiful introductions to the crew,
beautiful loyal few a loyal fuel oil. Phew

now it is him in a close-up, now the Tube
pipes him aboard in ventuplicate—Hey, Rube!—
as if there came rising to meet you,
out of the depths of time,
out of the La Brea tar pits,

this pained, voracious, brea-breathing Thing.

Can it be just Bob Hope,
surfacing like a jolly periscope?

O Canada O Greylag O Great Blue
heron or whale or goose or caribou
O lords and angels of migration, you
slumber among the Lagunaware unaware.

My opposites across the concourse hold
Brobdignagian snifters up,
deliberately, soberly. Ayup
Depth, body, bouquet. A better terrarium.

A plutocrat among them. Tweeds and jeans.
Diversified portfolio of gardening machines.
Chard-cherisher, cos-cossetter,
setter of mole's molestable table of greens.

The Garden Center clerk deployed to fill
daffodil-dogs and majolica-croc crocuses uses
white, violet, strawberry-colored rock.
Great vats of cobblestone and amaryllis.

And there's a sideshow. There's a Living Craftsman.
He does Huck Finns. He does Huck's fellow raftsman.
He wears an eyeshade like a gangster's draughtsman
and holds a dental drill, and in his hand

vanilla-colored scrimshaw minstrels stand
banjoing. Do you like them? Cougars leap
and jacktars dance, and wagonmasters whip
triplescoop conestogawagons up.

A spindle with a butterfly motif
sits cheek-by-jowl with Ahab Come To Grief.
He shows the agony in fiendish detail.

This is the way the whaleroad and the whale,
four oarsmen and a peg-leg legend end.
Take notice. Price an item. Be a friend.

Curio-user and curio-user
drift outside to the indoor street.

Demonstrators demonstrate devices.

Ekco! The last of the Beat Beat-
rices rices
rutabagas erasers and raw meat.
What an amazing feat.

Gimmicks and fripperies. It's downright canny.
Our turn to play trinketer and nanny
and kowtow, and keep quipus, and climb ropes.
Our turn to do deep-dyed horoscopes.

No more Golconda. No more pouring pigs
and flooding caissons and upending rigs
into the deep sea floor

Now it's Manaus burrowing to pour
huge footings for the skylines of desire.
Now it's the Indus' indus-
trial trial by fire.

DOGS' GOLFBALLS

```
AsForFactIHope
IComeDownForIt
Fourteensquare
AsAtSomeNovaya
PalatinskWhere
ASakharovDoing
Dimensionality
Investigations
PositsTenExtra
OnesInstressed
IntoEverything
AndProvesItOut
Experimentally
ToHisAmazement
```

A. B. GIAMATTI'S
INAUGURAL TOOT


```
OKTodayImDoing
BaseballAndThe
MonroeDoctrine
SoListenUpCame
OnTheMayflower
FloraDiMaggio&
BuiltTheBronx&
PlantedTheLand
WithSeethrough
ShimmerOfMaize
WhileTheThrogs
NeckTollBooths
ProsperedCause
ThePeopleMoved
Mountains&From
TownToTownSome
NewJitterWasIn
TheWindBlameIt
OnMaeWestOrThe
RexMaysAirShow

HouseRuthBuilt
OutOfAlienCorn
BallJournalism
ShudderedLikeA
Threshingfloor
AHurricaneASea
OfAgitatedFans
ButThatsNotWhy
```

ZachWheatsJive
&DaveWinfields
Chaff&Backtalk

Waver&GoSilent
Now&ThenTyCobb
GrrsAndJimRice
GrrrsRightBack
ButThatsNotHow
GodSteppedInTo
InventBaseball

NoSirItWas1954
Giants&Indians
TitansOfOldFor
Ever&Ever&Then
HistoryAndThat
GentlemenIsWhy
ItIsAKingdomOf
AngelsAwaiting

WillyTheSayHey
KidFieldsLikeA
GallopingDream
StopsDeadWhips
BackDobysLiner

LAMENT

There was a lad from Shropshire.
Lads to him were Scripture.
       Lads to him
       Were Seraphim
In antique Dantesque rapture.

Poor bugger. Stuck in Shropshire.
He doted on such sculpture
       As Elgin found
       All sprawled around
The Pnyx and ripe for sponsor.

He's dead now, lad from Shropshire.
Time was, he would have topped your
       Guinness up,
       And pledged a cup,
And stood you to a drop sure.

No more dumb rhymes for Shropshire.
No more strange spates of Bob's-your-
       Uncle an-
       Tiquarian
Palaver with the tapster.

Not all the clods of Shropshire
Can pressure him to laughter
       Or longing now,
       Nor Bion's plow,
Nor Cotter Mulkin's heifer.

JAPANESE FISH

Have you ever eaten a luchu? It's poisonous like fugu, but it's cheaper and you cook it yourself.

You cut it into little squares as fast as possible but without touching the poison-gland. But first, you get all the thrill you can out of the fact that you're going to do it. You sit around for hours with your closest friends, drinking and telling long nostalgicky stories. You make toasts. You pick up your knives and sing a little song entitled "We who are about to dice a luchu." And then you begin.

MAGNIFICAT. BRAVE CAT
AT SNIFTER FISHBOWL.

for May Swenson

Mmm, just might.   Minnow a
moment   now here
now   nowhere
tower a moment enlarged, like a   heretic
cataract plunging unchanging, like a cat's-eye
scatter, like a deco   herence, a
re fracting flaw.   There's half
the attraction: eye,   the ethereal, shot
unscathed into   lithosphere, swims!
has a Kitt Peak   vision, is a dis-
location, like the   starfish maw
catapultable out. Palomar! the proffered paw
widens and the sum of
hun-
gers
beg-
gars
Gar-
gantua's and you arrive
up to your ears in a handstand on one claw.

POEM TO BE TYPED ON A DONOR CARD

GentlesWhereas
TheDoublebreas
tedItemICameAs
HasNoSandfleas
LesionsOrIdeas
ForEvasiveMeas
uresDoYourBeas
tly&SeemlyBest

ItemMyPancreas
ItemTwoCorneas
Demounted&Reas
sortedCool&Eas
yAsDinos&Rheas
IntoTheLaBreas
MiniSanAndreas
&TheVastUnrest

CARGO CULT OF THE SOLSTICE
AT HADRIAN'S WALL (December 1988)

```
OTinyBombOTiny
BombWhatGangOf
MadmenMadeThee

OMiddleeastern
MasterpieceNoT
NTBetrayedThee

OEensieWeensie
IndyCarOCreamy
HalvahCandyBar

SeeEvenMrMovie
StarMakesFaces
ToDissuadeThee

IfEldAcquaints
TheElderlyWith
Frailty&Terror

ThePresidentOf
MegabucksFinds
Payable2Bearer

LiningsInLifes
Overcoats&Anti
DagoAnecdotes&

SummersBunchOf
HadjiiotesJust
HaddaBeAnError
```

```
OCheerfulnessO
WholesomenessO
AmityONiceness

OInfoInHisGrip
AttainingRegal
Impreciseness*

HeTakesTheCake
ForKindnessYet
290PersiansGet

NotOneSpasmNot
OneWetTremorOf
Thinktwiceness
```

*This form is recommended for beginners. It is as simple as it looks. Fourteen characters to a line. Difficulty arises only when a footnote is required. Then the poet must contrive a thirteen-character line in place of the canonical fourteener, so as to leave room for the asterisk. Most poems in the form evade the difficulty by doing without footnotes, save for poems like this which are designed to be put in textbooks.

READING THE FACTS ABOUT FROST
IN *THE NORTON ANTHOLOGY*

"Lover's quarrel" hah.
Little domestic
Eichmann in puttees
claiming he simply
had a taste for spats.

This was a real Scrooge.
His son killed himself.
Wait till you hear what
Mr. Thompson told
Mr. Ellmann. That's

all I know and all
I need to know. Frost
was a pig to his
wife, children, colleagues
and biographer.

So don't get suckered,
Undergraduates.
Like by the poems.
Like by sycophants
or apologists.

We can instruct you
also about the
Galapagos: "an
island group in
the Caribbean."

TELEMETRY BEFORE IMPACT

Fact: Large parts of Times Square are to be demolished and rebuilt in time for celebration of the Columbiad in 1992.

(the expanse of sidewalk)

A mass of savages. A pair of glasses.
A protozoa population crisis.
Clean slate and a phalanx of kazoos.

A potentate in carnival regalia
Plays pylon and panjandrum to the traffic
Debouching from a towering garage.

They told him this would happen in Columbus.
They told him to get back up off the canvas.
God's avalanche, the Ace of Dames approaches
Wilder than the Godiva of the Luge.

It's like a Steinberg. Only it's enormous.
It's oceanic. Even in the onrush
St. Diatom premeditates the whitewash,
St. Jeroboam bodes the vernissage.
O monument and sacrament and snowjob!

Totaled again. Braille billboard that she was.

(the expense of spearmint)

The dumpster and the dowager. Two stooges
Auditioning for dingbat. Not a chance.

The monumental Macy's-Day masseuses
Have galvanized their straphanger corteges
Into a hangdog shamble through the glitz.

Demimillennial expos in contraption.
Demimillennial thinkpiece out for bids.

Averted from the hadj, ensconced askance
Where lapsed therapsids scumble to the loge,
The mailbox mounts unshakable safari
Beneath his hat, in hatchet-faced repose.

He budgeth not to infiltrate the fury
Or ruminate the worm of circumstance.
He grudgeth not the flatness of the badge.

(the explicit statement)

Sensation. In the boîte around the corner
Sacred to the apostles of Le Boxe,
The novelist has punched out the director.
Their film is getting noir and going nowhere.

A cabinet of two-bit Howard Hugheses
And marinated Moho-maharajahs
Negotiates the marginal provisions
Of an escape clause in the tablecloth.

The bankable preadolescent bombshell
Dissolves placebos in her Shirley Temple.
The stuntman knows a goodie. Waxes Roth.

The monkey wrenches, thrown into perspective
As icons in the Nevelson decor,
Do such a job of looking nonobjective
They ought to get an Oscar for it. More
Mousse for the little lady. Waxes Roth.

The stuntman hunches forward and explains it.

He wishes he were talking to a mailbox.
He wishes they had given him a mailbox
To satchel, like De Niro in *Mean Streets.*

(the exploited starlet)

The emptiness is staggering, but staggers
On, through the stult and dundancy and heat.
The badlands knuckle under. Golden logos
Follow the flag. The product is complete.
The pinball in the basement skips a beat.
The mountains have a message on them. EAT.

The line around infinity approaches
St. nothing for his autograph. They meet.
She poses for some 40-second sketches.
He comes up with a title for them: "St."

She stands, in each, transformed into an object
Transformed into the person of its dreams.

She is the adulation of the lamppost.
She is the Duke of Hydrant, full of hemes.

She christens him St. Monolith der Mahler.
St. einberg of the emptiness. She sighs.
Are we the muse? the medium? the model?
Or nothing but a mailbox in disguise?
It's OK, she's wised up, she gets the message.
He doesn't have to act as if she mattered.
She goes all brave and squinches up her eyes.

He gives her a brassiere. She starts to bawl.
He puts his arm around her. Call me Saul.

(theoretic framework)

He puts a finger on the false horizon.
He puts a sidewalk on the window shade.
He draws her over next to him and shows her
Something in a toque, at a parade.

And how to let a mailbox be a mailbox,
And how to let the landscape have its tantrum
And lie there all exhausted in a heap,
And how to set a table in your sleep
And leave it there, to teeter with its platter
Until the waiting radiator utters
The crucial, terse, insinuating "st."

(the exploded notion)

Embarked on his blue-chip itinerary,
His holiness the horizon undergoes

48

The agonies of absence. Is she true?
He sends a wire. A lot of wires. A slew.

Her mother the Madonna of the Rockers
Had wanted a Rockette, but there it is;
You give them what you can: a set of feathers,
A little verbum sap about the biz.

And she herself? Ecstatic. Like an empress
Exemplifying transport on a barge.
She likes it here. She likes the Egg McMuffin.
She likes it when her friend the sidewalk artist
Transmogrifies the logos on the placemats.
She breaks up into giggles and conniptions
And squiggles and contraptions like a dope.
Oh dearie me. Historical convulsions.
Oh dearie me. Great gales and parking systems
And pyroclastic stratamatic fits.
She holds herself and howls until she splits.

(theodicy of the Abbie of the LEM)

Far from the madding franchise, at a table
Above the fair Potomac sits assembled
The legendary sachem of the tribe.

But it would take an artist to transcribe
The setting. The Colonial appointments.
The cobwebby display case full of jerseys
Dating to his great days as number one.
The back wall with its classical medallions
Like something from the sub shops of New London
Or half a quadraphonic speaker set-up
Or decorated patriotic hubcaps.

Pillar of smoke by day, and what is this?
Insomnia ensepulchred but serving
As distant-early-warning pyramid
While out the other window the bald eagle
Spreadeagles where he batters at the porthole
To bring to his progenitor's attention
A mighty confluence of telegrams.

(the Endowment enters)

They send an emissary for an artist.
The emissary chortles and absconds.

They send an emissary with an escort
Of samurais in samite. Shall these bronze
Originals get grungy and go green?

They send a squad of missing persons experts
Careering in a tinted limousine.

They send for the Endowment. An engraver
Had better get these likenesses and soon.
The eagle is in desperate condition.
The diagram the Rosenbergs were fried for
Appears above his noggin like a notion
Occurring to a bird in a cartoon.

(the endorsement shortened)

Manhattan. Five blocks south of a McDonalds.
The missing emissary counts his change.

And bides his time. His counterfeit accomplice
Has passages and passports to arrange.

He saunters up the avenue for breakfast.
The sunlight in the sidestreets is tremendous.
The hilltop where the distant vision grazes
Bobs like a mere meniscus of the henge.

The pavement is in factory condition
And shimmering from sea to shining sea.

So why not. He initials it. "St."

GASTARBEITER

There was an old woman from Szechwan
Who worked in the suitably Brechtian
  Town of Stettin
  Where she ran a canteen.
Or was it a woman from Szczecin?

No, this was a woman from Szechwan.
She went around kvetching in Quechuan.
  Philologists think a
  Lost tribe of the Inca
Reside as high lamas in Szechwan.

They came to the mountains of Szechwan
To study *Du C t de Chez Swann*
  And Melchior's question:
  What time is the next one?
And Leda's: why don't we go chase one?

Should Yeats have attempted to hatch one?
Should Christ have turned left at Saskatchewan?
  The track of Big Bird
  Is erose and absurd.
The trackers morose and Masaccioan.

LAST STRAW

IHaveNoTimeFor
BanterSirIAmAn
AncientMariner
MyShipWentDown
ICausedItsLoss
TheyTiedMeToAn
AlbatrossItIsA
BigPelagicBird
QuiteWholesome
IfAdministered
InternallyLike
ChickenSoupNot
TopicallyLikeA
StupidPoultice

SCAT

```
RepeatBuhTenTo
TheNthTimesAnd
ThenGoBuItsThe
CompleteJohann
SebastianBachB
MolMesseInBing
CrosbysVersion
&ItzhakPerlman
UsedToRattleIt
OffToHimselfOn
BusesWhenHeWas
Only2InPlaceOf
OverTheRainbow
WhyNotMeAndYou
```

THE DUKE OF IPSO'S ECOLOGICAL ECLOGUE

Mignonne, allons voir si la rose . . .

Within this balanced zoo,
green plants produce O_2.
A dollop of O_3
eventuates, and we
step out into the sun.
It's destiny, Mignonne.
The animals implore
the elements, "O for
a draught of Hippocrene
O wait O sweet sixteen
make it an *eau-de-vie!*"
And here you come with five-star Hennessey
in bottles just like everybody wants.
Delectablest of intoxicants,

let's you and me go see if the rosé
is ripening OK
and what these connoisseurs
and customers of yours
are up to when they go
two to the fifth, in slow
procession to the fields.
The midnight vineyard yields
a rush of oohs and ohs.
There is a coal that glows
downcellar, and the rows
of ripenings repose
like negatives of emblems of the sun.
O infinite. O one-and-only one.

TROVES FOR THE NATIVES OF 1992

Higgledy piggledy
Fifty Columbuses,
Fifty times richer in
Trinkets and beads

Couldn't provision the
Quinquecentennial
Memorabilia
Business's needs.

Arawak maidens in
Motherly attitudes.
Miniconquistadors
Mounted and spurred.

Bric-a-brac bins where a
Guatemaltecan can
Purchase a brace of his
National bird.

Product of Pakistan.
Product of Hungary.
Look! It's a caravel
Lighter than snow.

Santa Maria! the
Options in schlockery!
Serbian Steiff and Mor-
Occan Lladró.

Ferdinand Merciful
Monarch of Aragon,
Isabel Bounteous
Queen of Castile,

Shall it be you, or a
Made-in-Rumania
Mesoamerican
Calendar-wheel?

Polyacetylene
Ponces and Massasoits.
Demimillennial
Tupacs. It took

Five hundred years to dis-
Cover the India
Label right there on the
Indian. Look.

JOSHUA HAS HIS DREAM

```
DeathToOrtegas
AhabEyeglasses
GunsBunsLuxury
&TheyPlayRough
Grammarschools
ClinicsAllThat
Infrastructury
KindOfStuffIts
GogToTheRescue
VivaAndHeRears
HisHorseComoMe
LlamaNoImporte
CallMeElHombre
XCallMeElNorte
```

SPIN CONTROL

```
OhHeDidDidHeOK
UseItLetHimSay
CrossMyHeartHe
DontKnowDiddly
InHisOwnYouMay
FireWhenYouAre
ReadyGridleyDo
ItOrScrewItWay
ThenWeCanPlead
TheIneptnessOf
HisIntrepidity

TaintTheNathan
HalenessItsThe
GGordonLiddity
```

STILE

There was an old woman who dwelt
In a shoe but it sweated and smelt.
　　　She moved to a suburb
　　　And dwelt in a rubber
But it was all surface. She felt

Fashionable but unposh
Barely a custom galosh
　　　To show for her labors.
　　　As bad as the neighbor's
Bad wife who got kept in a squash.

Why can't she be Mrs. The Gipper
And live in a Tiffany slipper.
　　　Why can't she throw stones
　　　And keep up with a jones
And be known as a fabulous tipper.

This here is a woman who slept
Ten to a wedgie and kept
　　　Patching the toe hole
　　　And needed a Mohole
To sop up the buckets she wept.

She wants a vast Malibu mukluk
With burglar alarms that go "Cluck cluck
　　　Caducket grawk beep"
　　　And the bedrooms so deep
In hi-tech trash-compacted-Mack-truck look

She'll have to camp out in the boot
Of Mick Jagger's Ferrari, the brute,
   Or go gadding like Zelda,
   Or splurge like Imelda
On spare pieds-a-terre, and commute.

She pauses and ponders. Boo hoo.
How corny life was, and how true,
   Back when she was thirty,
   A dowerless, dirty
old woman who lived in a shoe.

OFFSHOREOILRIGWORKER
HAMMERKLAVIERSONATE

for the piano of
G. W. Beiswanger

```
Few&Far
        Few&Far
TheVisitations
OfTheAngelsAre
OrGodCanDoThem
In5SecondsFlat

OyVehInAManger
MyDoppelgänger
ISawAStavanger
Gaspipeflanger
HittingInAnger
AtACoinchanger
RatatatatatTat
PourBienRanger

ThereWas5Kr&He
WasItsClaimant
&LikeARafaelIn
FlamingRaiment
HeLaidOn&IDare
NotScuttleAway

OrWasItWitness
WasIMadeToStay
WatchingANorth
SlopePetrotech
```

nocratStripped
DownToSkivvies
AndAStetsonHat
WreakHavocInAn
OsloLaundromat

InAParisianGer
shwinTimeAtBat
HeWasDr&Badhat
Ludd&Mustanger
Anthemarranger
&Cashboxbanger
AHuger&Oranger
NadiaBoulanger

&HisMagnificat
ReverberatedAt
WavelengthsFar
&FewAndFar&Few
AsIfHeReckoned
OrAsIfHeKnewOf
OmensOdiousBut
KeptOnDrumming

&KeptTheGlobal
Infrastructure
HummingTheDark
PetroleumChrys
anthemummingUp
UpToBeBeckoned
IntoFlameHeWas
TheMadmanOfThe
NorthSeaWreck&
Troubleshooter

OfTehuantepec&
StoodHis10SqFt
OfBurningDeck&
WouldaBinABlow
TorchAnySecond
OnlyTheNornsGo
MistyAtHisName

ChristItWasOdd
HowLogyIBecame
AmidCacophony&
FlyingPlumbing
Apocalypse&Him
WereNeck&Neck&
BedlamHadIts2d
2dComingComing

LIKE DOTTED SWISS (FROM A BOOK OF UNRETOUCHED PHOTOGRAPHS OF THE PATTERNEDNESS OF THINGS)

for Amy Clampitt

White on green. If a microphotographer froze
this lipid at that angle. In those throes.
Or it's a satellite image. Something Castro's
hidden in sheds. Or it's Mies van der Rohe's
planet at last, and the highrise greenbelt boroughs
teem. But it's a caterpillar I

almost grabbed. We were ersatz braceros.
Headachy drenched green Chula Vista bean-rows
Taller than us for miles. This wasn't Thoreau's
greens patch. This was America's preteen heroes'
"war effort." And there were wasps like Zeros
buzzing the weird-shaped immigrant *pomodoros.*
And the beleaguered Alien Property Bureau's
Duce gave us a pep talk. We were pros.
The wasps were our ichneumon banderilleros.
Pretty white beads on green. Pretty as pharaohs'
viscera-boxes. Or a Mikado's inros.
Poor catafalque of would-be butterfly.

Better to be blobs and squiggles, chis and rhos,
white buff apricot cadmium mauve rose,
dotting the air in a weedscape of Corot's.
All flak and rapture. Beauty that must die.

Not this trompe l'oeil. Arlington. Book of rows.

NINETEENFIFTIES
VOGUE RORSCHACH

BecauseAWriter
ChancedToOffer
APhotographerA
HintNamelyHand
MarianneMooreA
TrulyHumongous
HatICanConnect
JohnJacobAstor
DiegoVelazquez
TheBeaverTrade
DeNirosBravura
DietrichFedora
&APoetPictured
InMyDictionary

HURRICANE ZEKE

for Swaggart

```
TicTicTicTicMy
EasterGrenade&
IAwaitTheBaton

CancunSheraton
IronFromOnHigh

Tetragrammaton
NeonWhizzingBy

CrownOfTVLight
&CoatOfSweatOn

ApocalypseAton
ementEmulation
Transmigration
WhatsMyCueATon
OfBricks&AnIGY
CollectibleOr2

NarySnakeToFry
OrBogToSquatOn


MyJobJob&Moses
JCInABedoroses
Headset&AnINRI
NametagUpATree
ItDontBotherMe
```

YourJobTerrify
EveryoneBigGuy
BadAsAkhenaton

BurgerUsLetFly
MeteorsSplaton

WhenPlainBaton
RougeBocaRaton
SunHitsYourEye
LikeA21Megaton
WedgeOfTomatoN
CheesePizzaPie
ThatsAMojoATon
TonMacouteDidn
BuyThatsAMoray
ByGumThatsATon
yBennettBuster
KeatonMXHidden
BallPlay&WeDie

AncientCluster

FeatheryDuster

YHWHTellethWhy

HARDEARNED OVERTURNED
CARIBBEAN BASIN STOMP

Blink. And the QE2 invaded Grenada.
Blazing away like Xmas. Broads and booze!
Fragments of a big brass figurehead, guess whose,
Lashed to the yardarm. Yankeedom had made a

Deal! Send me your Derek Walcotts your Vada
Pinsons your Harry Belafontes and your Rod Carews—
Quid pro quo for the juiced-up jet-set refuse,
The ruck of Uncle Slambam's neatsy nephews
I dump on your quaint ancient quays and queues.
Deal! lady with a ganja lemonade a

Grade-A grenadine grog and a contac fuse.
Deal! player-to-be-named-later in the Orlando Cepeda
Marianne Moore Bob Vesco Howard Hughes
Meganegotiation. Whatcha fraida?
Liberty-gibbet she loaded. Send canoes.

THE NEW REPUBLIC IS INFURIATED
AT THE NEWS COVERAGE

Teletype-music. OK, Maestro, hit it.
Chug chug chug chug chug, but the way they've split it
Into its drumbeats and re-edited it it
Dances like a machine-gun. Like a bird.

Two sentences. Ten seconds of Mirages.
The fashionable condos on the plages
Precipitated into their garages
Like slats into a trash can. Now this word.

The roteness. That's what gravels Marty Peretz.
Some namby-pamby in a trenchcoat ferrets
Out a Mirage'd size-seven and that's Eretz
Israel. That's the wrap-up. That's absurd.
Bittabup bittabeep bittaboop it's . . . Anchornerd

And a ten-second summing-up commences.
The policy of state and its defenses,
Shall go the way of last year's Lech Walesas:
Flashcard among a thousand bright unblurred
Experiences to be monitored

To jazz, when we have crisply disinterred
The Year That Was on January third.
No wonder Marty flares and Marty winces.
No wonder he says nothing that convinces
The cameras to backtrack. Now this word.

CATALOGUE RAISONNÉ OF
MY REFRIGERATOR DOOR

for Joshua Starbuck, master of montage

A Caledonian megalith.
A tinted bather from Cape Ann.
The 1937 kith
and kin of a Kentuckian
beside their Model T sedan.
The Celts. Who set me this arith-
metic of icons? Who began
by pasting in Bob Dylan? Zith-
erpicking rhinestone charlatan.
He tries to be American.

Who tries to be American
as hard as him? Not Aly Khan.
Not George F. Babbitt the Zenith-
ophiliac Zenithian.
As sure as God made Granny Smith
a pricier-sounding product than
the Winesap or the Jonathan,
there is a mystery and myth
to being an American,
and being an American

compounds it. Kurosawa-san,
steady my Nikon while I pan
across the porches of forsyth-
iabedizened Mattapan
in search of . . . dot dot dot . . . the plan,

the weltanschauung, the ethnith-
ifying principle a pith
helmeted Oxbridge fancy-dan
could pounce on like a fiend from *Ran*
and authenticate forthwith.

The cromlech beetles o'er the frith.
The ultimate American
possession rattles his Kal-Kan,
Prince, you're a prince. A dog a man
can talk to. What this caravan
of adumbrations and antith-
esises panteth for is Dith
Pran and the long-lost Mrs. Pran:
Far-fetched, tenacious, captious: fan
tabulously American.

DAME EDITH'S HUNDREDTH

```
YoHoUpSheRises
OffSheMorrises
AuxPiedsBrisés
LavedInCerises
AndAmbergrises
FiftyAmnerises
SitLikeLorises
RasAndOsirises
AlysAndIdrises
DimTheirKrises
AndPowerCrises
OhRitasOhRisës
BatThoseIrises
Jig!Spin!Shine
```

FIFTY YEARS OF NO GEORGE GER- SHWIN RAG

```
HeyWizUp&Doing
Rise&ShineHoDe
HoingDoUsRhine
StonedRodeoing
BeSwankSproing
SproingCiaoing
TaingHeyBroing

Dipfandangoing
IntoTheOngoing
GringoBongoing
AsASaloonGoing
HonkdomYoyoing
ToAConcertoInG
ForGrodyGoOink
```

FIFTY YEARS OF NO GEORGE GER- SHWIN RAG PART TWO

```
YabaDabaShtick
SavedUsInTheNi
ckelodeongoing
19TeensSoDoing
OrgyPorgyMeans
PopBopTop40ing
Hullaballooing
```

Neooratorioing
BacheriniBoing
BoingEvildoing
Schlockatooing
RagAsIfWeThrew
3Kisses&APoing
EnFaceDesDieux

THE WORD

(fugue on a theme by Dugan, a theme by Stevens)

Word was that what Word was
      would be first.
Reared back for the wild weird
      outburst,
Chaos, impatient, agog,
      heard
what the great name uttered.

Let it be with it. Wow. What it
      was was
      the the!
Everything anything, Alpha, Omega,
theirs! on a first-name basis! Get this free
      introductory the-
ology starter you name it you take it, all
hell and the kitchen sink at your beck and call!

The discount coupon. The servomotor. The larch.
The spectacles on the kerbstone after the peacemarch
and the right front wheel still spinning on the Le Car
and the bonze in the El Al also "create facts."
Stride into the donnybrook of molecular impacts.
It is as America's only purely
original living poet already
said: the the is the.

Suzerainty is impositable in this nominating-convention hooha.
Notable moments though in the general plethora.
Socrates and Li Po

saying ta ta to τω τω.
Sartre doing his uttermost Zero Mostel.
Hubble describing the gavel as God tries
to get word in edgewise.

WASHINGTON INTERNATIONAL

You notice them at check-in. Power. Dough.
Securing the cachet of their dispatches
With miniature touch-tone satchel latches.
Riding the tiger, going with the flow.
A naked envy flares in me and catches
Who manicures, who burnishes, who thatches
These bronzed embodiments? I know, I know—
Too dumb to trust with Momma's kitchen matches,
Let alone World War III. But there attaches
To them and their assumption such a haloed
Ritziness . . . And to find one in my row . . .

The stewardess has catered me my trayload.
I buddy up with dumbshow down-the-hatches.
A conversation bumps along in snatches.
The Plexiglas is bright with microscratches.
We monitor the murmur of the payload
As if our slice of Fortress U.S.A. lowed
Homeward the way the herds of Thomas Gray lowed
Homeward, and there were centuries to go.

PLEASURES OF THE VOYAGEURS

Into the limitless nowhere. Lightly canoeing.
Day sultry. Me desultory. Toing and froing
testing the bottom for bass, or in fact just yoyoing
aimless assortments of ornament up and down.

Very encouraging soundtrack, once you get into it.
Whole Canadian laid-back percussion section.
Woodpecker, marshhen, dittybug, loon, frog.
Sidemen, all of them, happy to just hit-it-when-indicated.

Like spending the afternoon with one of those riff-it-yourself
    records.
Bunny Berrigan Band on a golden oldie.
Only the lead madman is absent, or sits obstinate.
He won't stand up to get "I Can't Get Started" started.
Why should he? Why should I? Why perpetrate
a Paderewski-at-the-outboard ruckus?

Cryptic and infinitesimal gunnel-thunks
like a dim rockbass bass to the ongoing bongoing.
What am I doing going boing boing?
Am I a mad baboon? I was suddenly pogoing
hugely over the lake I was flap-flap-flapping
like eohoopoes afire, like a red-eyed screecher
out of an early-sixties Fright-Nite feature
hitting itself and croaking "Dumb! Dumb! Dumb!"

It was, you might say, galvanizing, this
demonstration of what the container meant
about "reapplications" of repellent.

I was the Living Dead on moonlight excursion
I was the Hunchback of Notre Dame in the Laughton version
with the canaille following and the bells echoing
I was the mass of scab velcroing and unvelcroing
slugwise forth I was everything (sproing sproing)
evildoing a nickelodeongoing
urchin ever befouled himself boohooing
home from the slobbering Roxy not to see.

Wouldn'a missed it for the world, not me.
It scared the Missus, damn near totally.
Wiser than Queequeg (and with fiercer tattooing)
is brave Nokomis home from his mosquitoing.

About the author

George Starbuck was born in Columbus, Ohio, in 1931, to a migrant academic family. In his mid-teens, he studied mathematics for two years at the California Institute of Technology. He also attended the University of California at Berkeley, the University of Chicago, and Harvard. He took no degrees. He was an agricultural worker, a military policeman, a fiction editor at Houghton Mifflin. He directed two of America's finest graduate programs in Creative Writing—at the University of Iowa and Boston University. He taught English and poetry for twenty-five years—one year at the State University of New York at Buffalo, then at the University of Iowa and Boston University. He gave poetry readings in nearly every state as well as abroad. Due to illness, he took early retirement in 1988. He was the distinguished chairholder in poetry in 1990 at The University of Alabama.

While at the State University of New York, Buffalo, in 1963, he was fired for refusing to sign the required loyalty oath. He initiated a challenge of New York's Fineberg loyalty oath law and was successful when the Supreme Court of the United States overturned that law. Also in the 1960s, he was an anti-Vietnam War organizer and activist.

His first book, *Bone Thoughts,* 1960, won the Yale Series of Younger Poets prize. He subsequently received a Guggenheim Fellowship, the *Prix de Rome* of the American College of Arts and Letters, and other awards. He was a fellow at the American Academy in Rome and later at the Rockefeller Foundation in Bellagio, Italy.

White Paper, his second book, set a standard for charged, edgy American political poetry. His next, *Elegy in a Country*

Church Yard, is the world's widest concrete poem. *Desperate Measures* tackled, with fine Byronic insouciance, everything. *Talkin B.A. Blues* is a book-length rhyming picaresque in rhinestone-sourdough style. In 1982, Atlantic Monthly Press and Secker and Warburg (London) published his new-and-selected poems, *The Argot Merchant Disaster.* That book won *The Nation's* Lenore Marshall prize, among others, for best book of poetry. He published two small books with Bits Press: *Space Saver Sonnets* and *Richard the Third in a Fourth of a Second.*

He was honored with the Aiken-Taylor Lifetime Achievement Award at the University of the South in Sewanee, Tennessee, in 1993. He died at home in Tuscaloosa, Alabama, August 15, 1996 after a twenty-one-year struggle with Parkinson's disease.